UNDER THE SEA

AN UNDER WATER ADVENTURE & COLORING BOOK

KRISTI TRIMMER

AlaskaWildandFree.com
KristiTrimmer.com

It is quite serendipitous to see the photographs I took as I traveled come to life as coloring pages in this book. I've taken countless day cruises out of Seward, Alaska to capture the pictures of marine mammals. Most of the coral reefs and fish were photographed in southern waters and at aquariums. I'm a huge animal and nature lover and enjoy bringing that wildlife to the pages of my coloring books.

I spent four years solo camping in National Parks throughout the U.S. as a travel writer. Never in my wildest dreams did I think my six-week adventure to Alaska would result in loving this state so much that I moved here. I'm an Alaska artist and writer, and I absolutely love it.

Alaska is my muse, her beauty my playground.

Follow my Alaska and travel adventures at KristiTrimmer.com and find stickers and magnets that match these illustrations at AlaskaWildandFree.com.

Thank you to my family and friends for supporting me as I've lived this life that is a little less ordinary, and a little bit more wild and free. ~ *Kristi*

TABLE OF CONTENTS

Bottlenose Dolphin

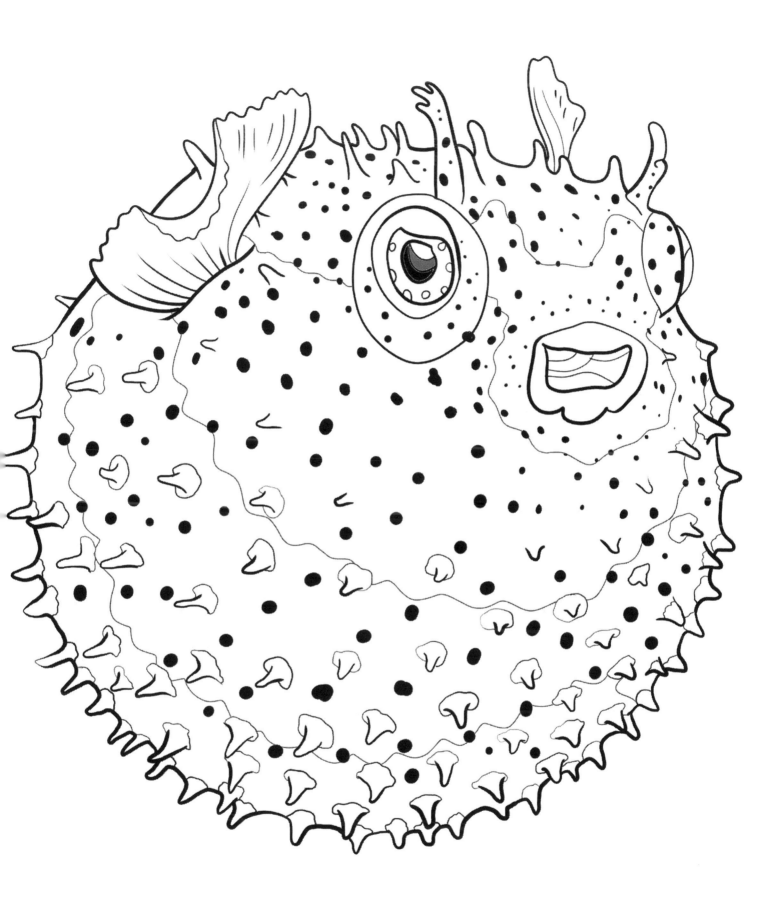

Balloon Fish

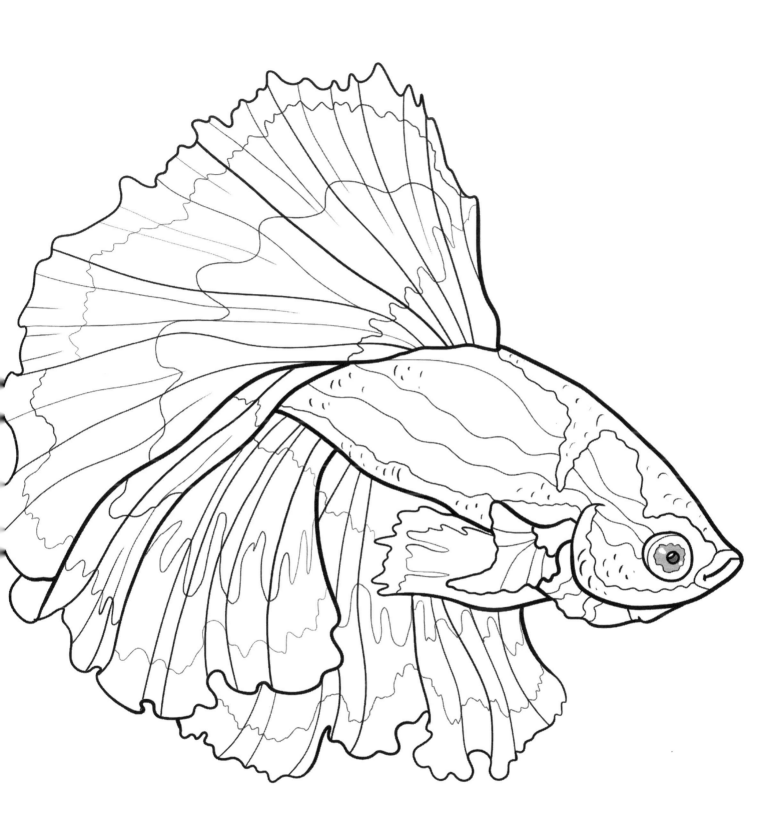

Betta Fish

Blue Tang

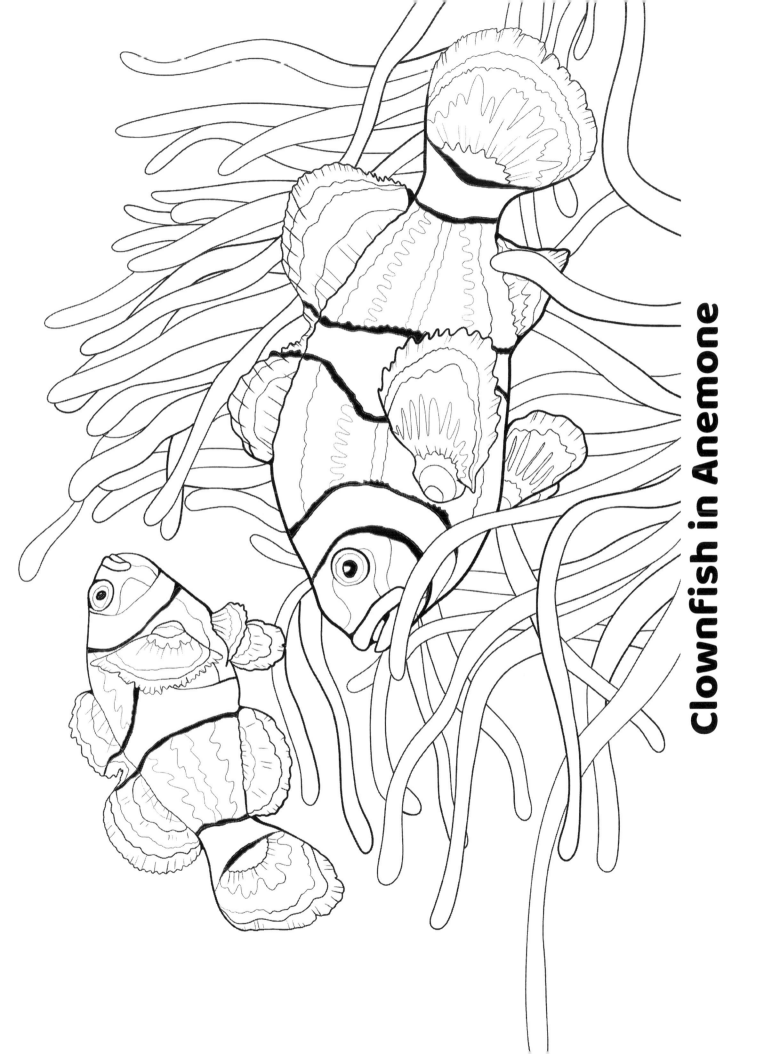

Clownfish in Anemone

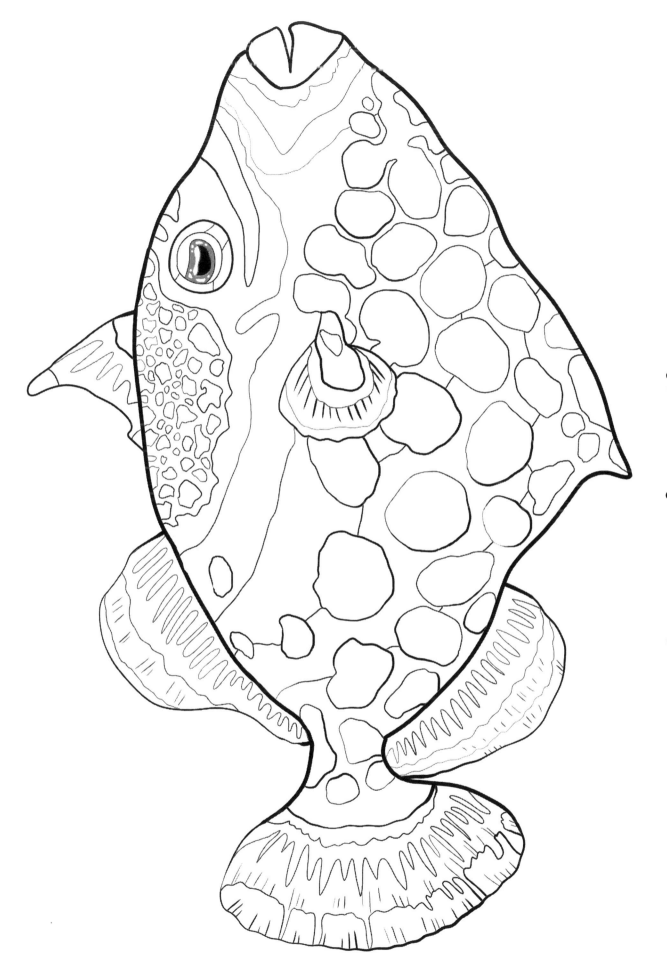

Clown Triggerfish

Coral Reef

Dall's Porpoise

Dungeness Crab

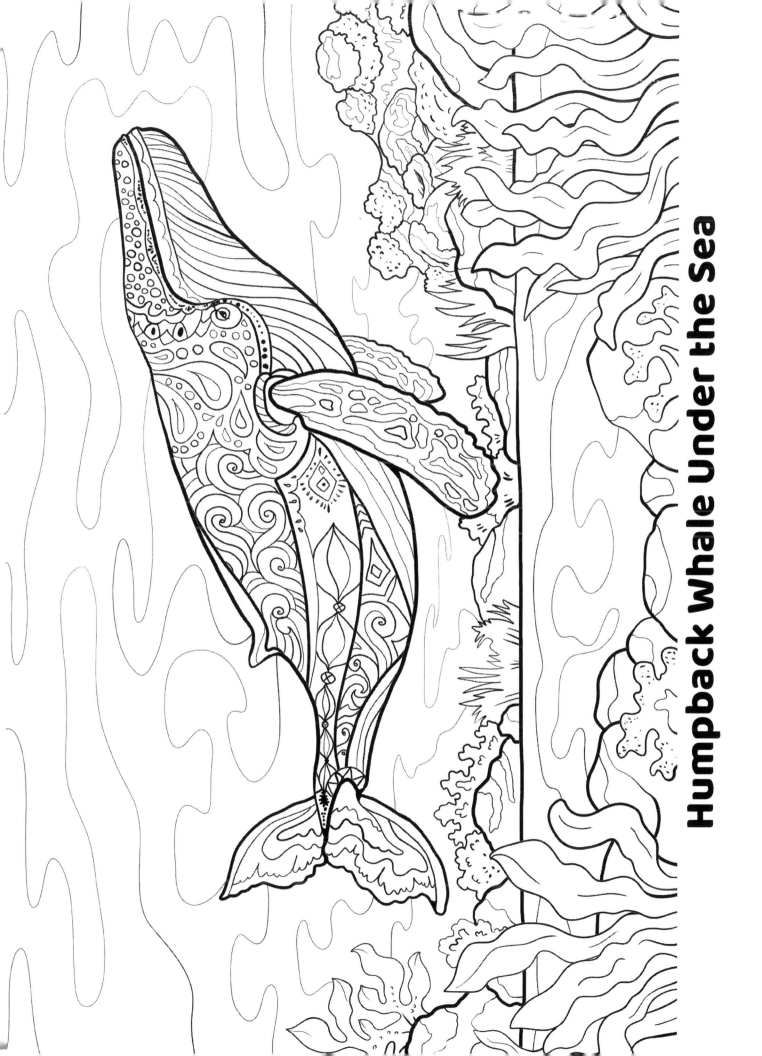

Humpback Whale Under the Sea

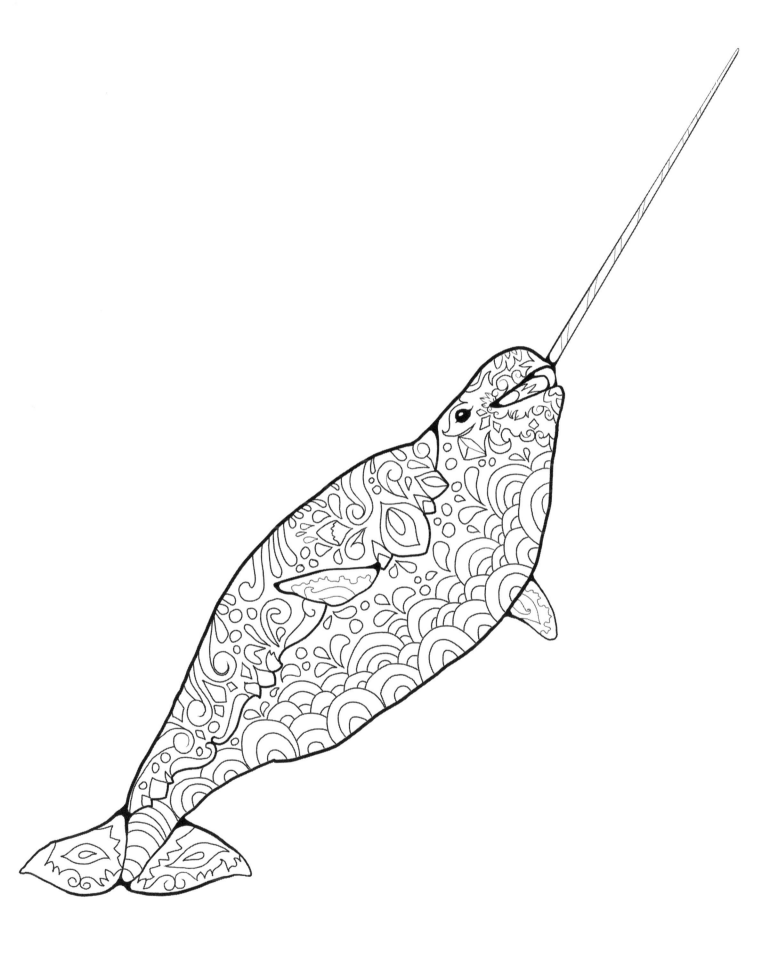

Narwhal

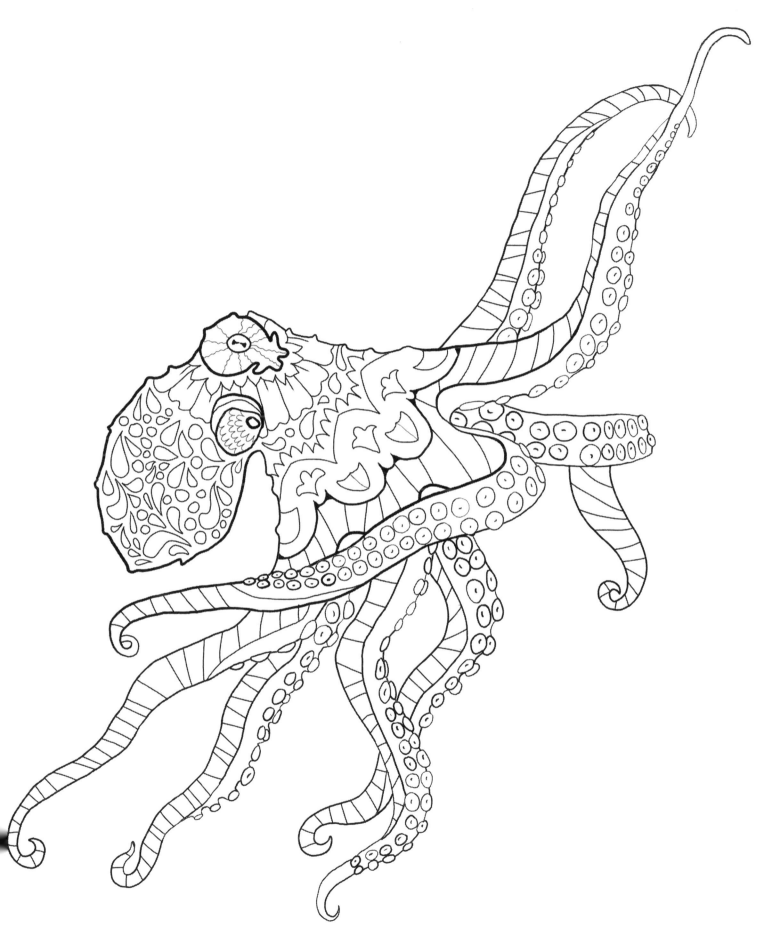

Octopus

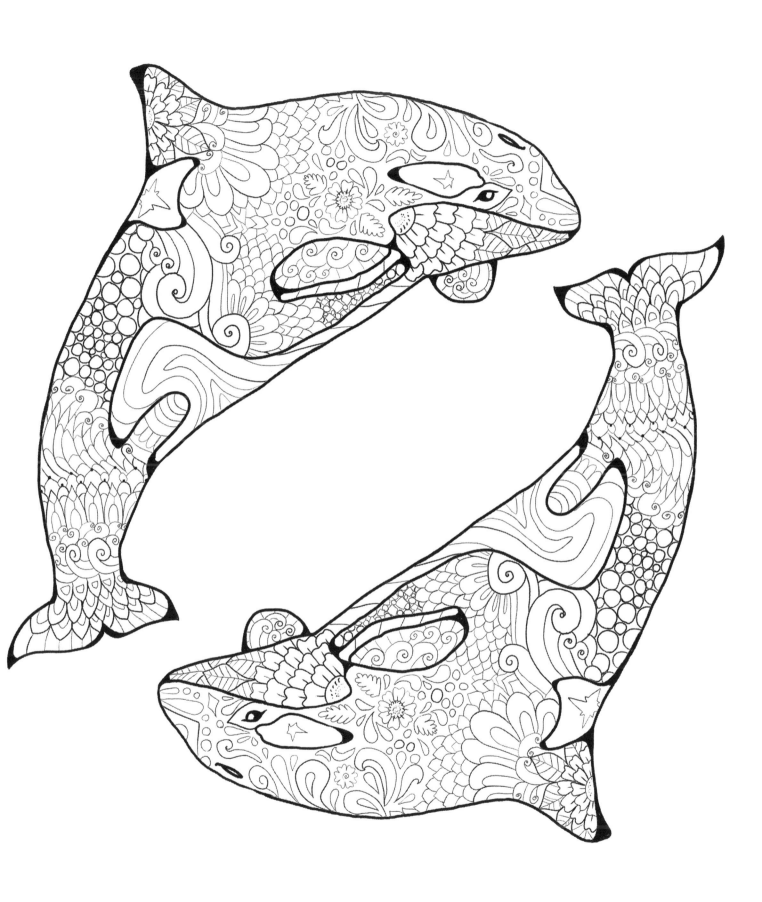

Orca Whales

Puffer Fish

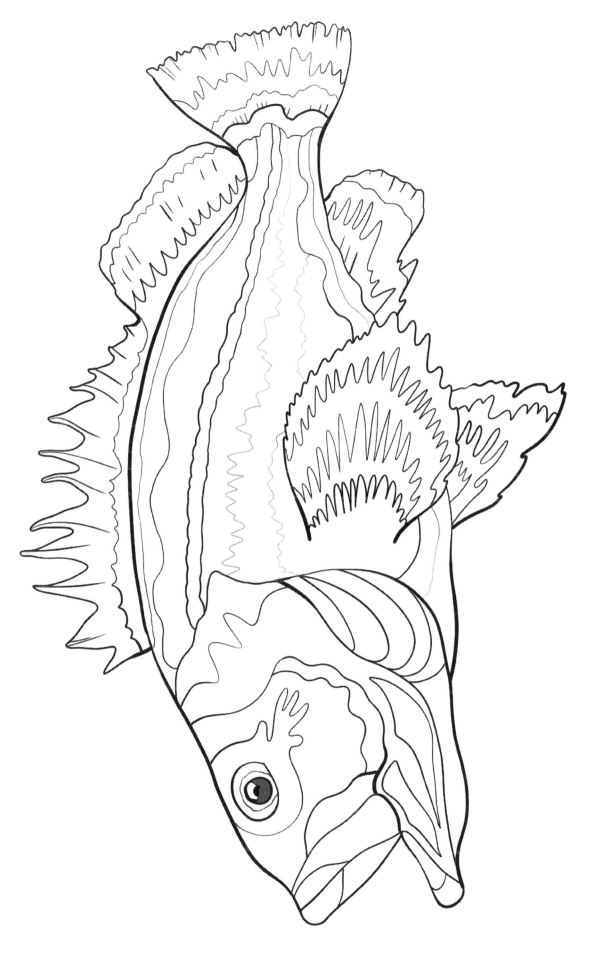

Rockfish

Salmon & Halibut in Alaskan Waters

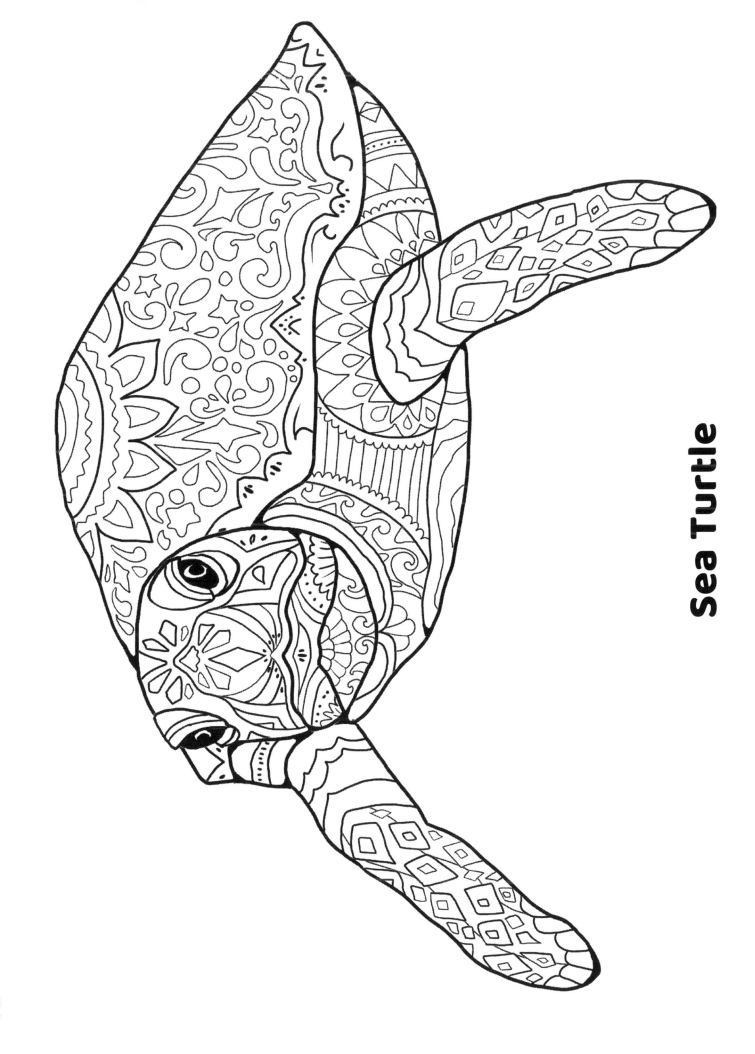

Sea Turtle

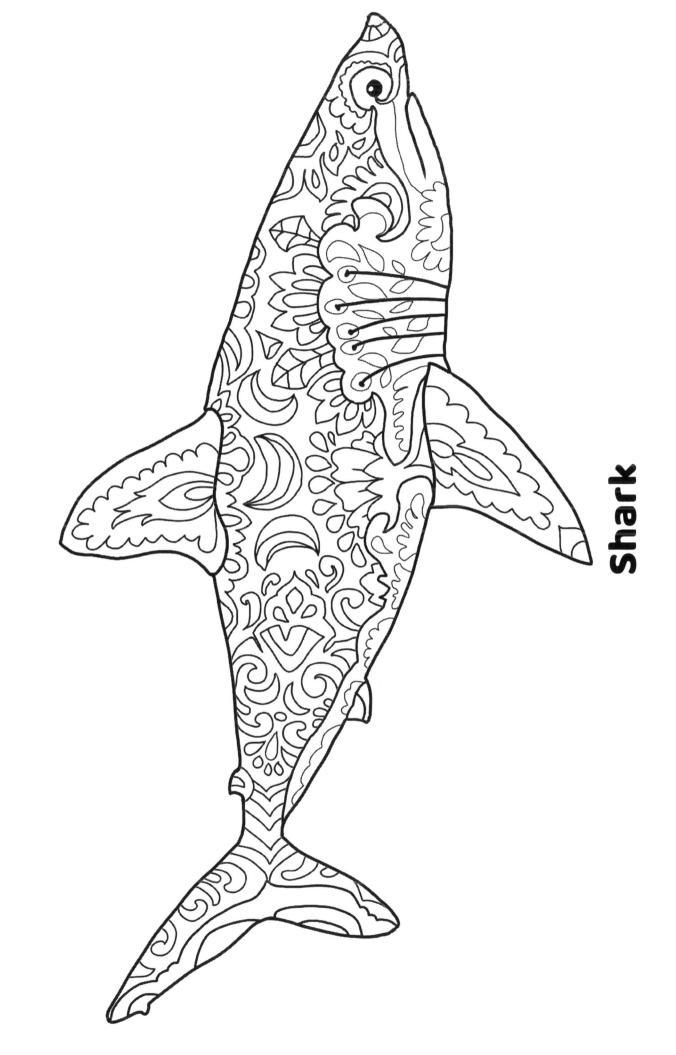

Shark

Starfish

Steelhead Trout

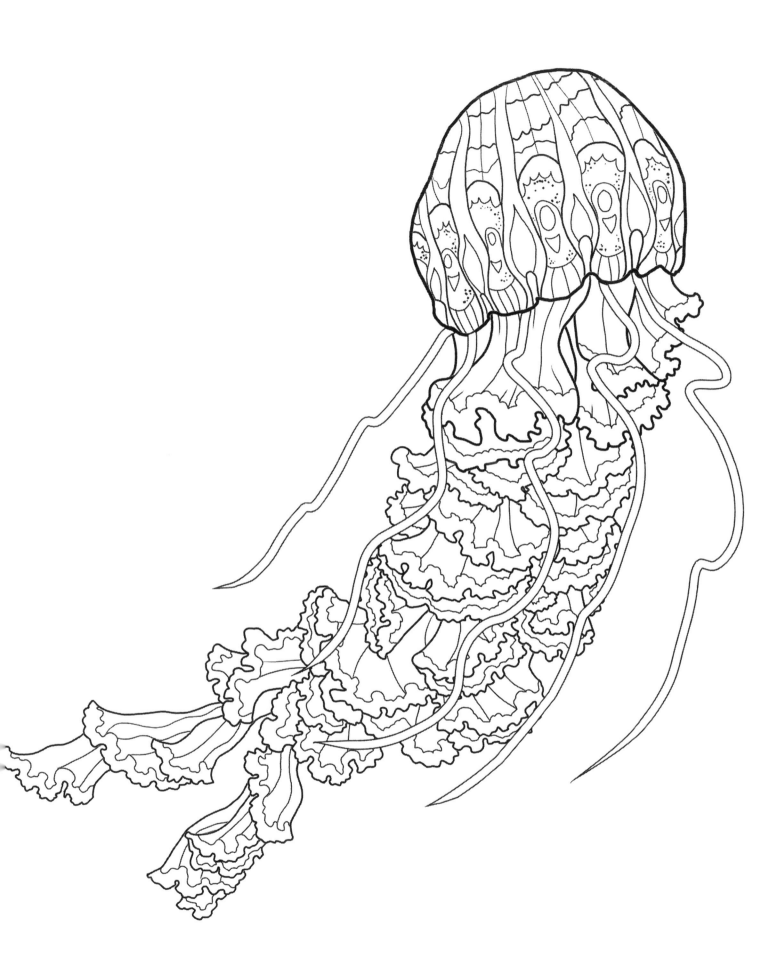

Tiger Mane Jellyfish

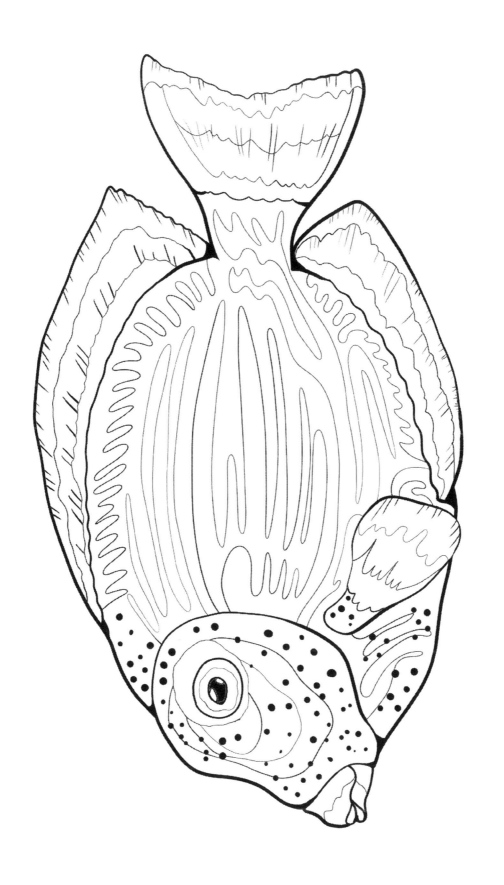

Yellow Eye Tang

38020774R00028